I'M THE
BIGGEST!
IN THE
PRAIRIES

LAURA K. MURRAY

CREATIVE EDUCATION · CREATIVE PAPERBACKS

CONT

4
Let's Explore
the Prairies!

7
Temperate
Grasslands

11
Tallgrasses and
Shortgrasses

14
Animals, Big
and Small

18
Full of Life

ENTS

20 In the Prairies

22 Word Review

23 Read More & Websites

24 Index

LET'S EXPLORE THE PRAIRIES!

The sun shines brightly in the blue sky. An American bison grazes in the grass. A small **calf** stands at her side. Use your binoculars to look at their shaggy coats.

calf - the young of a bison

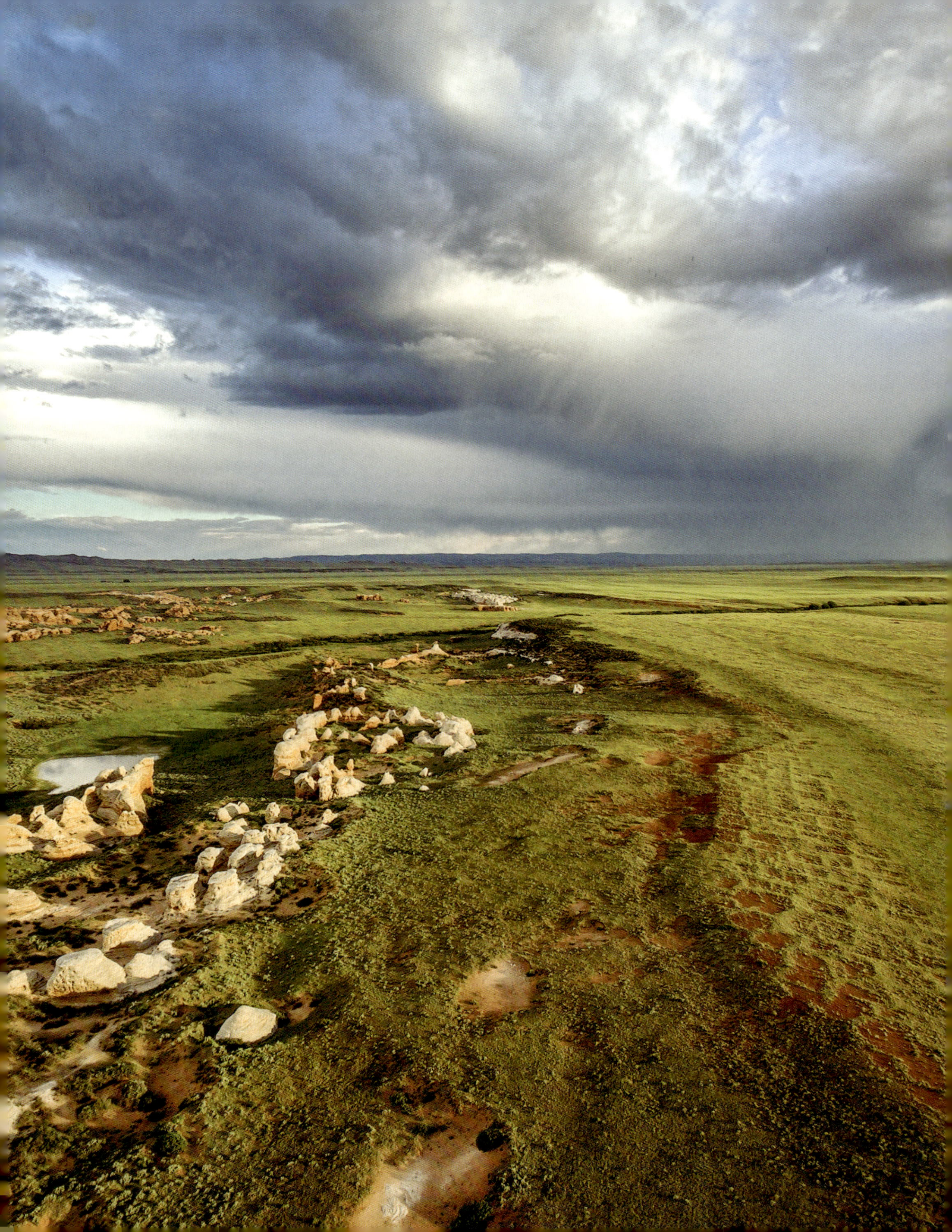

Temperate Grasslands

North American prairies are **temperate** grasslands. These areas have few trees. Around the world, temperate grasslands have different names. They are called velds in Africa. In South America, they are called pampas.

veld

pampas

temperate - having seasonal temperatures, with hot summers and cold winters

A steppe is a type of temperate grassland. North America is home to both steppes and prairies. Steppes have short grasses, while prairies have tall grasses. Steppes receive less rainfall than prairies.

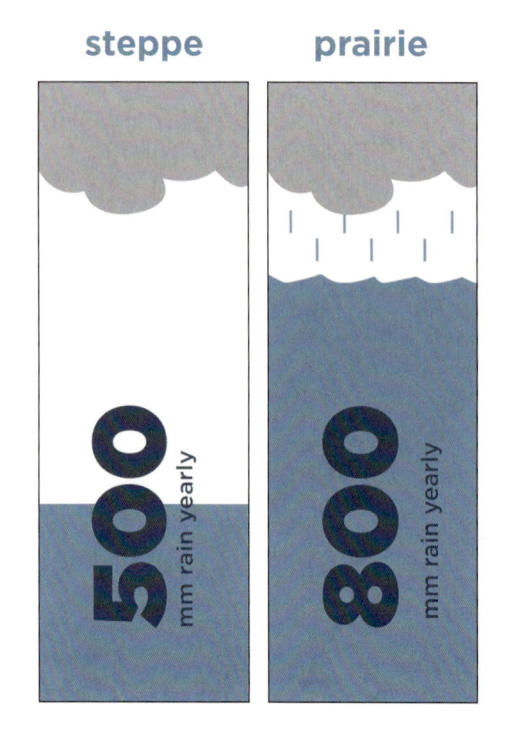

steppe — 500 mm rain yearly

prairie — 800 mm rain yearly

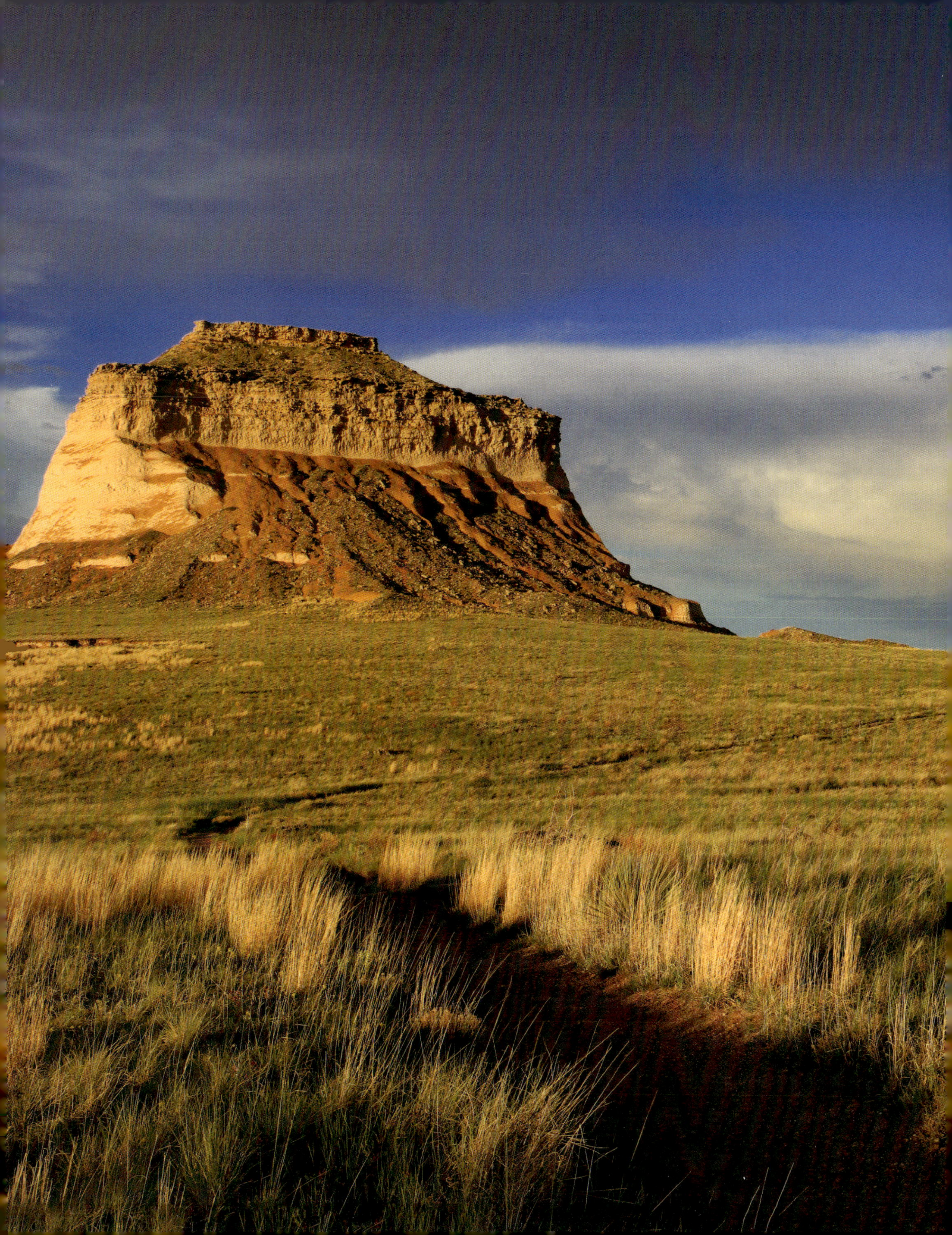

tallgrass prairie

shortgrass prairie

Tallgrasses and Shortgrasses

The eastern plains of the United States contain tallgrass prairies. Grasses may grow taller than five feet (1.5 m). The western plains contain shortgrass prairies. Grasses there are generally less than two feet (0.6 m) tall. The prairies meet in the Midwest. There they form mixed-grass prairies.

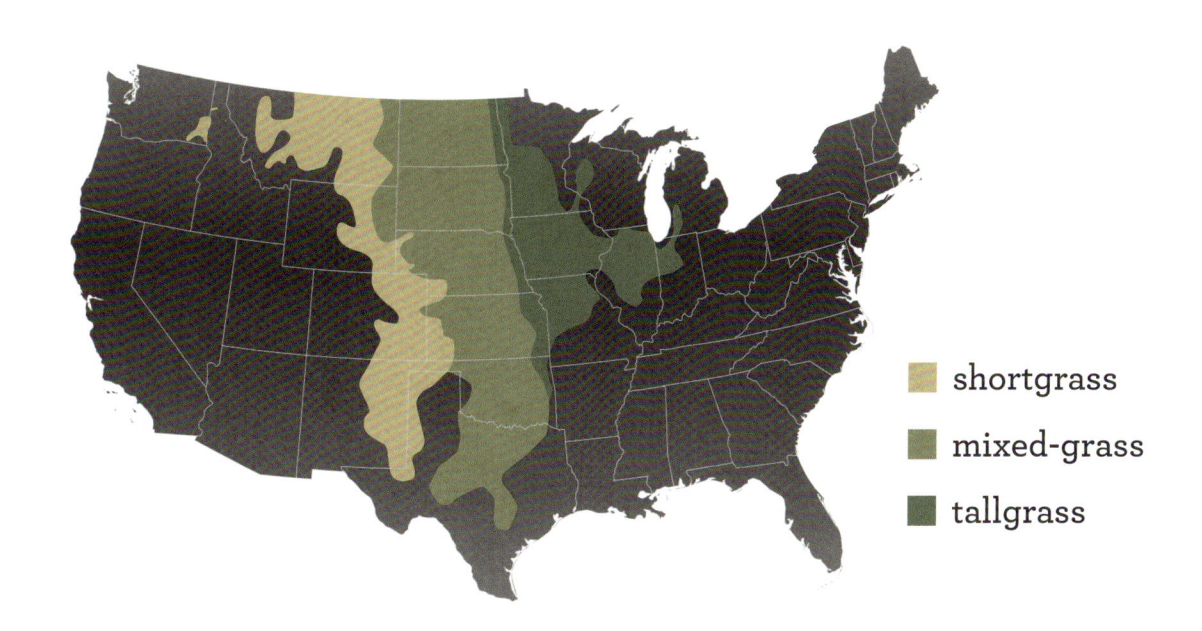

- shortgrass
- mixed-grass
- tallgrass

Many prairie plants have long roots. This helps them survive dry conditions. Leadplant (opposite) is a low shrub. Its roots reach more than 15 feet (4.6 m) deep. They spread five feet (1.5 m) wide.

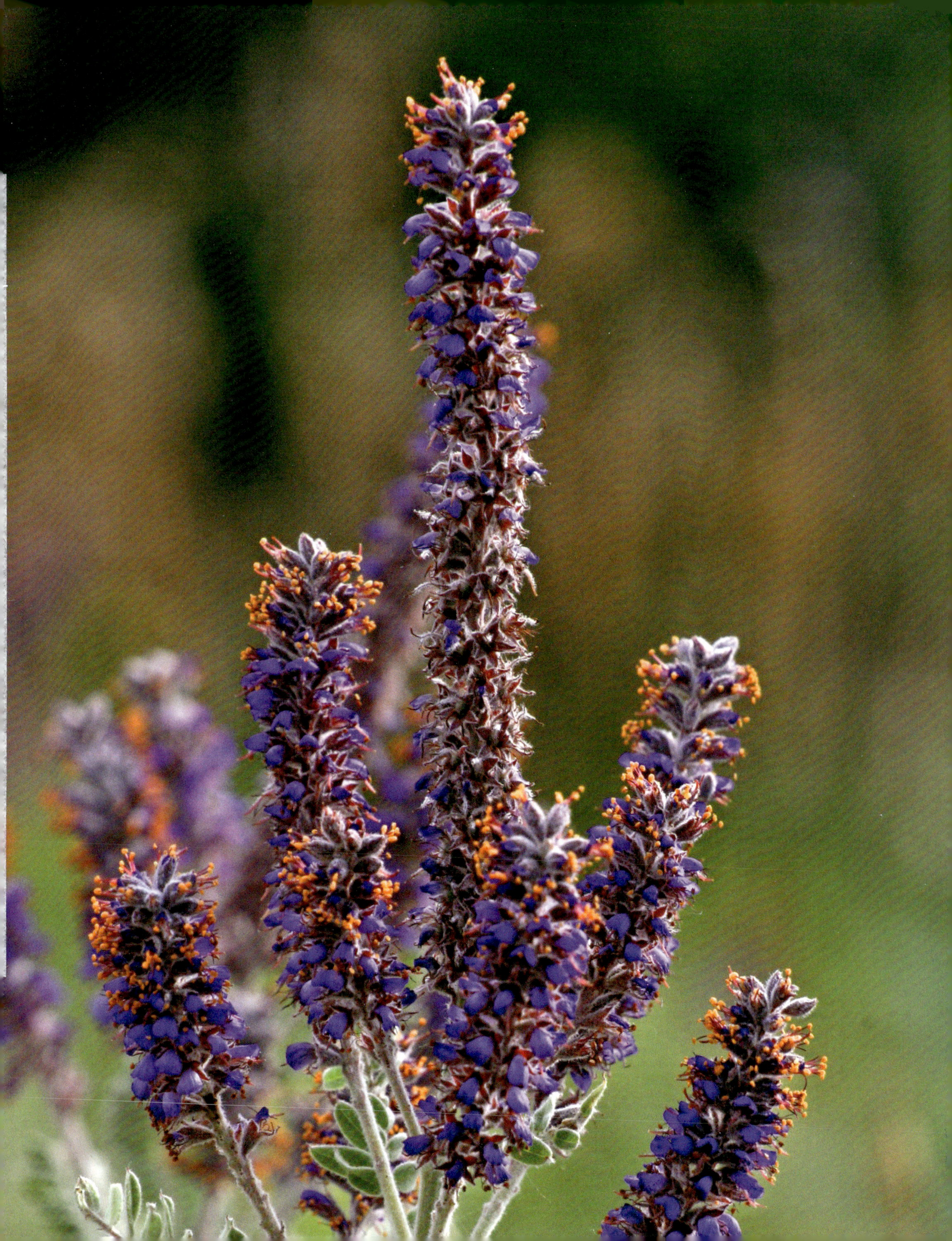

Animals, Big and Small

American bison are the largest land animals in North America. Males can be more than 2,000 pounds (907 kg). These huge **mammals** were hunted until they almost died out in the 1800s.

size comparison

weight comparison
~ 2 grand pianos

mammals - warm-blooded animals that have hair or fur, give birth to live young, and feed their babies milk

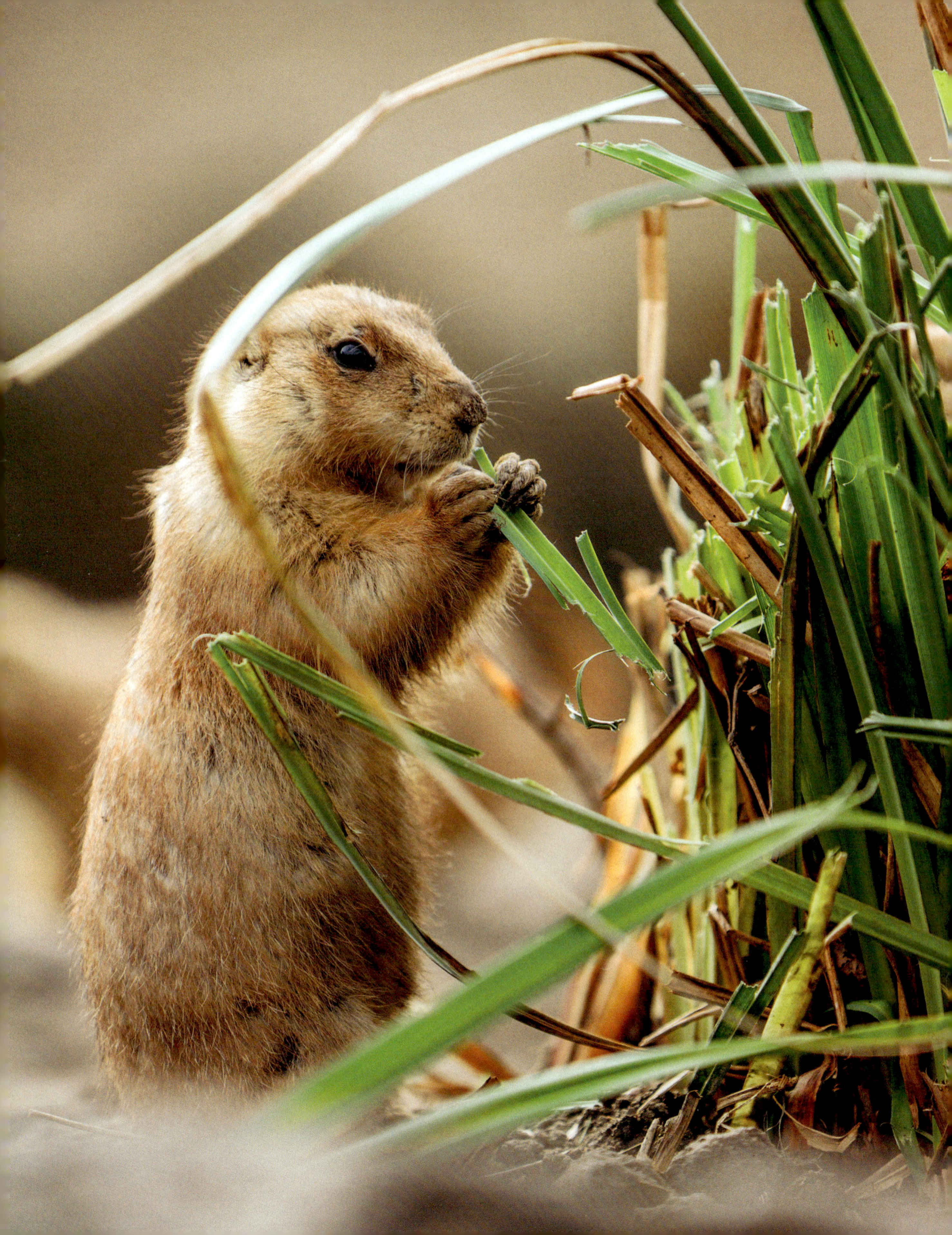

Prairie dogs are much smaller mammals. They weigh only about four pounds (1.8 kg). Grasshoppers are even smaller. People may consider prairie dogs and grasshoppers to be **pests**. But they are both important food sources for prairie wildlife.

pests - animals that cause problems for humans

Full of Life

From grasshoppers to bison, prairies are full of life. What other amazing things can you discover about these open, grassy places?

prairie falcon

pronghorn

coyote

American bison

prairie dog

grasshopper

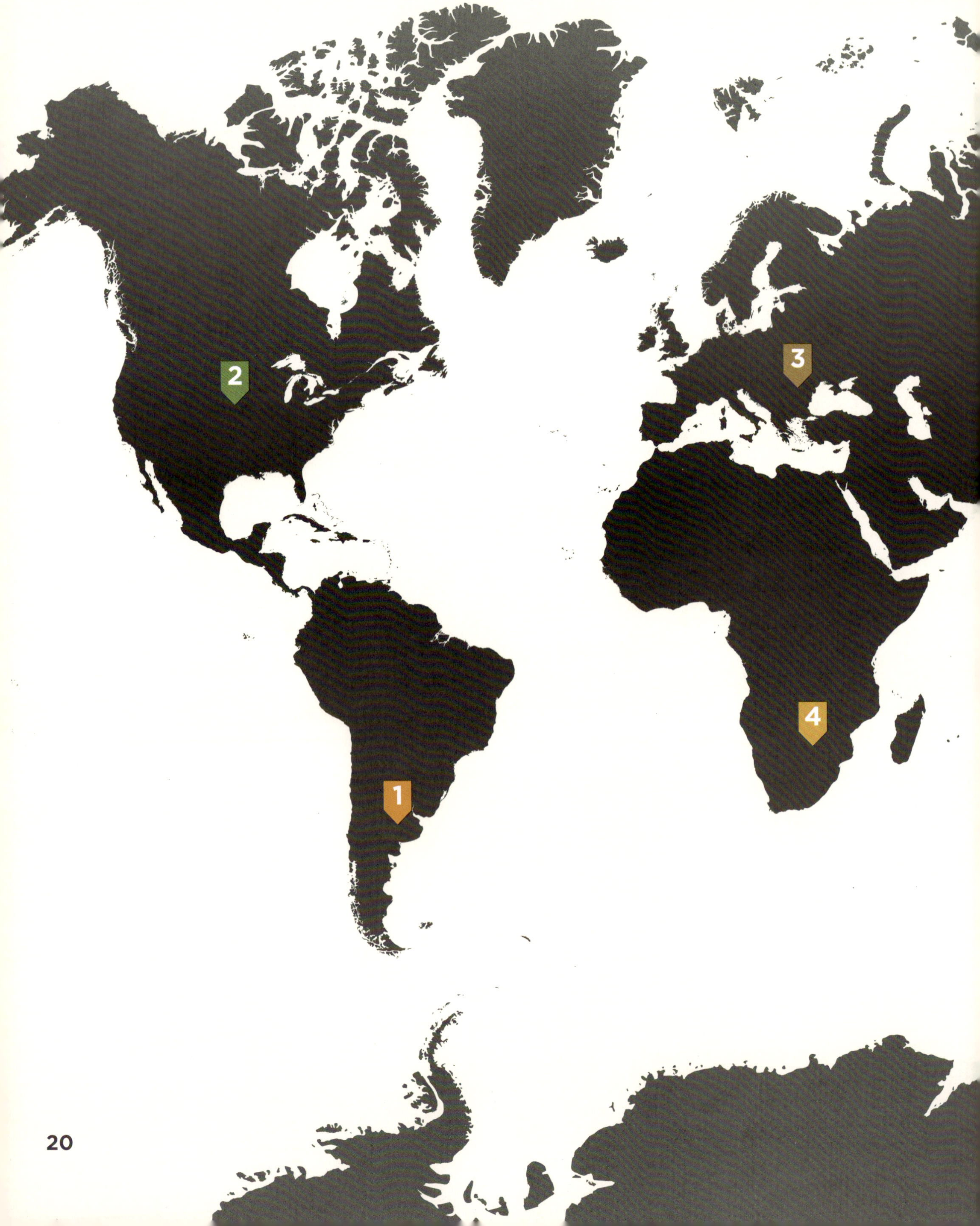

2
3
4
1

IN THE PRAIRIES

Temperate grasslands around the world:

4 African velds

3 Eurasian steppes

2 North American Great Plains

1 South American pampas

21

Word Review

Do you remember what these words mean? Look at the pictures for clues, and go back to the page where the words were defined, if you need help.

calf page 5

mammals page 15

pests page 17

temperate page 7

Read More

Bowman, Chris. *American Bison*.
Minneapolis: Bellwether Media, 2015.

Riggs, Kate. *Prairies*.
Mankato, Minn.: Creative Education, 2010.

Websites

National Geographic Kids: Prairie Dog
https://kids.nationalgeographic.com/animals/prairie-dog
Read all about the tunnel-digging rodent.

World Biomes: Grassland
http://kids.nceas.ucsb.edu/biomes/grassland.html
Learn more about the different types of grasslands.

Note: Every effort has been made to ensure that the websites listed above are suitable for children, that they have educational value, and that they contain no inappropriate material. However, because of the nature of the Internet, it is impossible to guarantee that these sites will remain active indefinitely or that their contents will not be altered.

Index

American bison	5, 14, 18	**prairie types**	8, 11
grasshoppers	17, 18	**mixed-grass**	11
leadplants	12	**shortgrass**	8, 11
names for grasslands	7, 8, 21	**tallgrass**	8, 11
prairie dogs	17	**rainfall**	8

PUBLISHED BY CREATIVE EDUCATION AND CREATIVE PAPERBACKS

P.O. Box 227, Mankato, Minnesota 56002
Creative Education and Creative Paperbacks are imprints of The Creative Company
www.thecreativecompany.us

LIBRARY OF CONGRESS CATALOGING-IN-PUBLICATION DATA

Names: Murray, Laura K., author.
Title: In the prairies / Laura K. Murray.
Series: I'm the biggest.
Summary: From shortest to tallest and biggest to smallest, this ecosystem investigation uses varying degrees of comparison to take a closer look at the relationships of prairie flora, fauna, and landforms.

Identifiers: ISBN 978-1-64026-063-4 (hardcover)
ISBN 978-1-62832-651-2 (pbk)
ISBN 978-1-64000-179-4 (eBook)
This title has been submitted for CIP processing under LCCN 2018938966.

CCSS: RI.1.1, 2, 4, 5, 6, 7; RI.2.1, 2, 5, 6, 7; RI.3.1, 2, 5, 7; RF.1.1, 3, 4; RF.2.3, 4

COPYRIGHT © 2019 CREATIVE EDUCATION, CREATIVE PAPERBACKS

International copyright reserved in all countries. No part of this book may be reproduced in any form without written permission from the publisher.

DESIGN AND PRODUCTION

by Joe Kahnke; art direction by Rita Marshall
Printed in the United States of America

PHOTOGRAPHS by Alamy (Steve Boice, Dr. Torsten Heydenreich, Joe Mamer Photography, Ivan Kuzmin, Marek Uliasz), Creative Commons Wikimedia (Gary Eslinger/USFWS Mountain-Prairie/Flickr), Dreamstime (Isselee), FreeVectorMaps.com, Getty Images (Danita Delimont/Gallo Images, Manuel Sulzer/Cultura), iStockphoto (AfricaImages, davemantel, debibishop, GlobalP, JohanWElzenga, Renan001, roberthyrons), Shutterstock (aarrows, Rauf Aliyev, Collins93, elmm, Frank Fichtmueller, Foto 4440, Erick Isselee, JackF, kojihirano, nighttman, Nisalwa Raden-Ahmad, ricardoreitmeyer, Weldon Schloneger, ShutterSparrow, Volosina)

FIRST EDITION HC 9 8 7 6 5 4 3 2 1
FIRST EDITION PBK 9 8 7 6 5 4 3 2 1